About the Author

David Lease is currently the United Kingdom Under 23 Team Director. Previously he held the positions of National Coach for the Western Region of the South of England and National Head Coach for Jumps. He represented Great Britain as a pole vaulter and also competed in the World Trampoline Championships. He was a team coach for the British Olympic Team at the 1992 and 1996 Olympic Games, but delights in coaching athletes of all ages. Some might say his specialities are jumps and sprints, but he prefers to be considered a coach of people rather than of events. He is the author of the official instructional book on Combined Events.

Photograph by Mark Shearman (Official Photographer to UK Athletics),
22 Grovelands Road, Purley, Surrey. CR8 4LA. Tel: 0181 660 0156

ATHLETICS IN THE NATIONAL CURRICULUM

Athletics has a central role in School Physical Education programmes. Athletic activities are one of the six areas of activities laid down at Key Stage Level Two by government decree. At Key Stage Level Three all pupils must be taught games, plus one full area of activity and at least two additional half units, of which athletics is one of five. At Key Stage Level Four, pupils must be taught a minimum of two different activities, one of which must be a game, and athletics is one of the remaining options open to teachers and their pupils.

It is vital for teachers of athletics to see the role and place of the sport in the overall Physical Education programme. The ethos and modus operandi pervading the total subject area is evident in the following extract from "The National Curriculum' (1994).

General Requirements for Physical Education

"Physical Education should involve pupils in the continuous process of planning, performance and evaluation. This applies to all areas of activity."

The essence, in reality, is a continuous process of "learning from doing", as the greatest emphasis is meant to be placed on the actual performance aspects of the subject.

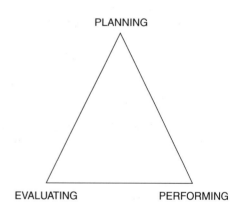

At Key Stage Level Three children should be taught:

a) To apply the techniques, skills and competition rules specific to the events.

b) The effects of taking part in the events in question.

c) To apply the relevant mechanical principles underpinning performance.

d) To apply and extend their techniques and skills to other events.

e) To take part in competitions and refine their performance.

At Key Stage Level Four children should be prepared to be able to:

a) Plan, carry out and evaluate an effective personal training schedule.

b) Master increasingly advanced techniques and know how to improve performance.

c) Apply the strategies/tactics in the events chosen.

d) Extend their personal capabilities and evaluate performance in the events chosen.

In putting together a programme of work, the teacher should ensure that the children are being educated towards:

What they should *understand* in athletics.

What they should *know* in athletics.

What they should *do* in athletics.

Any planning work done should indicate:

a) How the lesson/session will be organised.

b) How the work will be adapted to meet the needs of the performers.

c) The content needed.

d) The resources required.

e) The chosen assessment indicators.

f) The safety elements to be considered, i.e. working environment, teaching methodology, material to be taught etc.

Athletics in Education involves two main concepts:

The ROOTS of

Running	**Jumping**	**Throwing**
arm action, leg action, body position, cadence	approach, take-off, flight, landing	transfer of weight, rotation, power application

The CONTEXT of

Running	**Jumping**	**Throwing**
Speed, distance, over obstacles, different terrain, in co-operation with others	Long, high, swinging combinations	Pulling, pushing, slinging, heaving

Runner	*Jumper*	*Thrower*

Throwing is important for its own sake. It is a core element for many other activities within the P.E. curriculum, particularly games.

It is vital that pupil involvement and activity is not sacrificed at the expense of the technical aspects of the events. It is also important that meaningful experience is afforded irrespective of gender across all four events. A major role of the teacher is to facilitate a maximum pupil activity and involvement as an aid to learning.

To quote from "Teaching Physical Education at Key Stages 1 and 2", produced by the PEA, NDTA and BALPE:

> "Designing and presenting simple *athletic* type activities is one dimension of successful teaching and learning. Children engage in activities and learn by doing; the teacher then needs to consider how children's performances in these activities can be made better or improved, to help children run faster (etc)."

> "The role of the teacher, therefore, is complex and crucial. (S)he will need to select from a variety of teaching styles and use appropriate strategies in order to achieve particular objectives. Children's needs will vary and the teacher will have to adopt different strategies . . . at times orchestrating . . . on other occasions giving children more autonomy to discover for themselves."

> "A teacher-directed, more command orientated approach would be more suitable, particularly in situations where technical competence in running (for example) needs to be developed. (At other times) it would be applicable to use more open-ended, questioning or guided discovery strategies (e.g. 400m hurdle stride patterns or relay baton exchange techniques). In essence, the teacher facilitates a learning environment where children are encouraged to THINK about what they are going to do, have a go at DOING it and then LOOK to see if improvements to the performance can be made. This represents a tripartite teaching and learning process . . ."

These instructional principles also hold true as sound practice in athletics clubs.

(This preface was written by Richard Simmons).

1. A PERSONAL PHILOSOPHY

Three requirements must be met if pupils are to learn:

FACILITIES — to allow the activity to take place.

TIME — to practise.

KNOWLEDGE — to understand how to progress.

In truth, the teacher does not actually have to be present for learning to take place, and teaching is not just the preserve of teachers. Give a child a computer and the software of a game and watch the results!

HOW DO WE LEARN?

Most movements are learned by trial and error, and all the results stored in the cerebellum (little brain) which is placed at the top of the spinal cord, just underneath the main brain. These movements can be called upon and tinkered with by feedback, so that we can reproduce them in different forms and different situations.

Consequently, it is important to build a large and varied store of movements to allow us complete control of our bodies. This is best accomplished when young — in the primary stages. Learning can then continue through into adulthood. We should not just learn, or simply try, specific movements but learn every possible movement. Why not learn how to fall?

Above all we should learn how to learn and learn how to work. We should not underestimate how long it takes to learn movements correctly. It takes us nearly two years to learn how to walk.

Many children are denied the opportunities to benefit from an education in jumping, which will limit their potential in so many other activities: because the teacher lacks confidence, or is not interested, or is even frightened . . . frightened of accidents, or even that their lesson will be a failure. It is important not to limit children's experience because of one's own prejudices.

Athletics, and in particular jumping, is an excellent medium for education to take place. If pupils realise:

MORE PRACTICE = IMPROVEMENT but:

MORE INTELLIGENT PRACTICE = EVEN MORE IMPROVEMENT,

then this is a lesson for life!

However, it is unlikely that pupils will realise the most efficient and effective form of movement for themselves. Therefore — read on . . .

2. ESSENTIAL INTRODUCTORY OBSERVATIONS

Jumping is an intense activity and can be very stressful. It should be practised only for short periods of time.

Jumping is a natural activity and the human body is designed to jump. However, that does not mean humans will naturally jump correctly! Children exhibit jumping during play, and this should be the foundation on which to progress.

For effective learning to take place the following are important:

The correct information needs to be understood by the pupil.

The subject matter should be appropriate to the age and stage of the pupil.

The most appropriate teaching method should be used.

Correct facilities and appropriate equipment must be available.

The pupil must enjoy the process, and the product of the process.

The pupil must be allowed time to practise; the pupil must practise accurately.

The pupil should practise regularly (consider optimum repetitions per session, and optimum rest period between sessions).

Sound and safe practices only must be used.

Activities which indicate to the pupils that they are no good should not be used!

Good teaching enhances an individual's natural talent. It does not stifle it. All students can be confused when too much detail is offered at any one time.

Whether a long jumper runs from 4 strides or 11 strides, or takes off at an angle of 17 degrees, is not what is important. The information in this book is detailed for the benefit of you, the teacher. It is not dogma. Please accept it as the first step towards what works for you and any one particular pupil - at any given time. That pupil may respond to an holistic approach or a regimented style. A little of both and lots of individual practice might be best!

The skill asked of you is to appreciate the individual nature of learning and to communicate the essentials to best effect. **These all require the teacher to prepare.** Good teaching means planning for maximum involvement. There should be little or no queuing. Good teaching means planning for 'Teaching for Understanding'.

NOTE:
Children's ability, especially their coordination, can be hidden by their lack of strength or lack of flexibility. Late developers often make super athletes. Therefore, patience is required. Late developers usually have long limbs!

Experienced teachers consider about five repetitions at each practice to be about right. After about eight rehearsals skill starts to deteriorate. Perhaps it is concentration that deteriorates.

SPRINTING TECHNIQUE
Sprinting plays such an important part in the jumping events that you are advised to study the companion booklet "How to Teach Speed Running".

3. INTRODUCTION TO JUMPING

This section is for all beginner jumpers, but the work should really be completed before the onset of adolescence.

It is impossible for anyone to express themselves in any medium without the appropriate 'vocabulary', whether it be verbal, written, artistic, musical or physical — jumping included.

This section should therefore be seen in the same light as teaching someone to read.

WHAT TO TEACH

1. An understanding of what jumping is.

2. All basic forms of human movement that come under the banner of jumping including:

Jumping from 1 foot to 2 feet
   left foot to 2 feet / right foot to 2 feet
Jumping from 2 feet to 2 feet (bunny jump)
Jumping from 2 feet to 1 foot, left & right
Hopping left to left / right to right
Bounding 1 foot to 1 foot, left & right.
Sequences of each, e.g.
  4 hops or
  4 bunny jumps.
Sequences of combinations, e.g.
  hop / bound / hop   hop / bound / jump
  hop / hop / bound   1 foot to 2 feet to 1 foot etc. (hopscotch)
Sequences of each completed with a steady, even rhythm.
Jumping with an appropriate arm action, e.g.
  bounding with a double arm action
  bounding with 1 arm back / 1 arm forward.
Galloping.
Jumping for distance.   Jumping up onto.
Jumping for height.   Jumping down from.
Jumping with good form.   Jumping over.
Jumping for accuracy.   Jumping into: water.

Jumping with actions while in the air, e.g.
  star jump
  tuck jump.
Jumping with the aid of a pole (boy scout vault).
Jumping from standing.   Jumping and throwing.
Jumping from a run-up.   Jumping and catching.

Landing safely.
Landing effectively
  ready to go again, or
  to stop still.

HOW TO TEACH

How one teaches these introductory movements may depend on the pupils' age.

Method 1

Children can be taught jumping as part of a 'Movement' lesson.

Challenges can be issued: Can you show me 2 different jumps? How softly can you land?

However, at some point the movements need to be learned and performed correctly rather than just tried. At this point the teacher might approach it as follows:

"John has given us an excellent answer. I think we should all copy John and learn his method. Let's practise."

Individual attention will need to be given to many pupils to ensure they are performing correctly — as in reading.

"Do you know the name of that jump? Well done! It is called a hop. Who can perform a hop on the other leg? Let's practise."

This method can be progressed to sequences: "Show me three different jumps, one after the other. Let's copy. Let's practise."

And so on –.

Required for 25 pupils: Hall or flat dry grass.

Method 2

Investigative or problem solving questions can lead to understanding, as well as achieving correct movement:

Try jumping without bending your legs.
Try jumping with bending your legs.
Which takes you further? Why?

Jump with static/swinging arms.
Jump off the heels of your feet.
Jump off the ball of your foot.
From a heel contact, rolling onto the ball of the foot, jump.

For older pupils:
What does your free leg do on take-off? Why?
Where is your bodyweight (centre of mass)? And so on.

Required for 25 pupils: Hall or flat dry grass.

Method 3

A rather more formal method, requiring more preparation, is to place markings on the floor.

Thin non-slip plastic can be cut out in the shape of feet and placed on the floor. Alternatively, feet can be drawn on the floor in chalk or paint.

The pupils jump from marker to marker, matching their feet to the markers. This method should be used as part of an activity circuit or as an activity station. The other activities may or may not be jumping activities.

Method 4
Adolescent and adult pupils can also appreciate a more formal 'copy an expert' method.

4. LONG JUMP

Long jumping can be taught efficiently as a class activity by splitting a large class into groups of 4/6 and providing each group with their own activity station. It can be taught in an indoor hall.

All children can long jump to a degree. Therefore, the immediate aim is to refine the activity rather than teach an unknown skill, which is the case in the other three jumps.

WHAT TO TEACH
A 'STRIDE' JUMP is arguably the best model to aim for eventually because it is effective and contains all the essential principles in the easiest format. The number of approach strides should approximately mirror the pupil's age.

Within that broad aim the following should also be included:

An accurate run up	A feeling of correct flight
Rhythm of take-off	How to land safely
Action of take-off	How to land efficiently.

THE STRIDE JUMP TECHNIQUE

Run-up

The start should be from standing — for accuracy.
The run should accelerate progressively until the last two strides.
The last two strides into take-off are made with a galloping (daa-de) rhythm.

Take-off

The athlete must jump at take-off, not just run off the take-off
board.

Posture .... natural, upright, head tall but not thrown
back.
Arms .... should be driven upwards — one forward,
one back.
Take-off leg .... should be extended explosively — downward and backwards.
Free leg .... should be driven upwards so that the thigh is at least parallel to
the ground.

Flight

Free leg .... is extended in a striding action.
Take-off leg .... is pulled through bent.
Arms .... are extended above the head.

Landing

Legs................ are extended together and kept as high as possible.
Arms .... are swept down and back. This causes the legs to lift up.
The jumper..... slides into the hole in the sand cut by the feet.

HOW TO TEACH

The best method of teaching the long jump is 'whole, part, whole'. In other words, pupils
have a go; then isolate and practise a vital element; then have another go trying to
incorporate the improved, practised part.

PROGRESSIONS

1. Have a go.

Method 1

In teams of 4/6, pupils have two attempts each. Measure each pupil's best attempt and add
all together to produce one distance for the team. The team with the longest distance wins.

Method 2

Better still: Zone the landing area with markers. Past the first line gets 1 point, second line
2 points, etc. Everyone has two attempts. Add up the total team points. The markers should
be positioned so that every pupil is able to gain at least one point.

Try again to improve the team's points and individual performance.

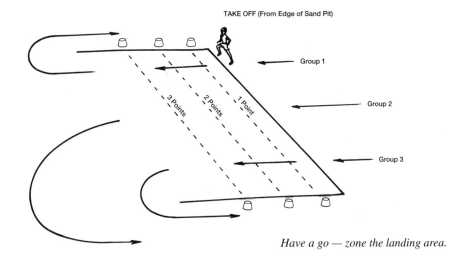

Have a go — zone the landing area.

Required   — large wide sand pit
              — dry take-off surface
              — cones or measuring tapes.

2. Develop a correct take-off action and correct take-off rhythm.

A problem which occurs with beginners is that they prepare for landing too soon, resulting in an incomplete take-off action.

Method:

In sequence: 'Gallop' over 3 obstacles and long jump.

To exaggerate the feeling of take-off, the pupil bounds over each obstacle. A short step is taken between bounds, so that the obstacle is cleared with the same foot leading each time. The take-off action is extended through the bounds, so that on the fourth bound (the long jump) there is a noticeable delay before the pupil pulls the take-off leg through for landing.

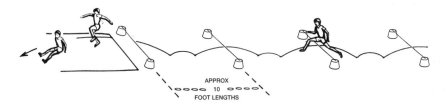

*Gallop over obstacles
and jump.*

The obstacle should be low - 10 centimetres. (Flowerpots with garden canes, or non-splinter equivalent laid across are ideal.)

The distance between each obstacle including the landing area should be approximately 10 of their own foot-lengths. However, experiment to find the most suitable distances for each group.

Required for a group of 5:
    one mat or sand pit
    3 canes
    6 flowerpots (10 cms. high)

3. Introduce a measured run-up

There are two methods of organising a measured run-up.

Method 1

Run back from the take-off area. A partner counts the strides and spots the footmark at however many strides is agreed, 10,11,12,13 or 15.

Advantages: — Quick and simple.

Disadvantages: — Athletes running in both directions on the run-up.
               — Gives no understanding of run-up construction.
               — Erratic results.

Required:
    Large sand pit.
    Markers for each athlete.

Method 2

Assemble the run-up gradually using the following format:

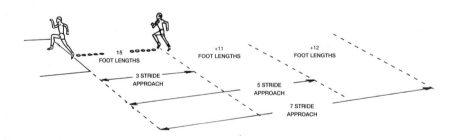

Measure back from the take-off area 15 pupil foot-lengths. Mark. From the mark run 3 natural steps and jump.

Measure back from the take-off area 15 foot-lengths and a further 11 foot-lengths (26 in total). Mark.
From the mark, run 5 natural strides and jump.

So:-

  3 stride approach = 15 pupil foot-lengths
  5 stride approach = 15 + 11 foot-lengths
  7 stride approach = 15 +11 + 12 foot-lengths
  9 stride approach = 15 + 11 + 12 + 13 foot-lengths
11 stride approach = 15 + 11 + 12 + 13 + 13/14 foot-lengths

Advantages
— This scale works for most pupils.
— Indoor mats can be used initially as an alternative to outdoor sand pits.
— It allows controlled practices.
— Understanding of run-up construction is provided in that the first steps taken are short and added strides are progressively longer.
— Standing start practice is ensured.

Disadvantages
— Some individuals find it difficult to fit (often the strongest). In which case revert to method 1.

Once established, this method provides an ideal practice situation:

From 3 strides, practise the correct arm action   — five jumps
From 5 strides, practise driving the free knee   — five jumps
and so on.

Required for a group of 5:
  one gym mat or sand pit
  one scratch line
  5 markers.

NOTE: Long, Triple and High Jumpers are not disadvantaged in any way by using an odd or even stride approach. Should you as the teacher feel an even stride build up is preferred then the scale advised is:

  2 stride approach = 10 pupil foot-lengths
  4 stride approach = 10 + 11 pupil foot-lengths
  6 stride approach = 10 + 11 + 12 pupil foot-lengths
  8 stride approach = 10 + 11 + 12 + 13 pupil foot-lengths

It is important to appreciate that these scales highlight a principle but are adaptable, i.e. a less than strong pupil may prefer to start 9, 10, 11 etc.

4. Develop a controlled/balanced flight.
Develop a safe and correct landing action.

Rarely are pupils in the air long enough to give them time to do anything constructive. Jumping up off a low step provides some extra flight time.

Method

From a short (five stride) approach (25/26 foot-lengths), step onto and jump up from an 'aerobic step' or gymnastic box top.
Land on two feet.

Practise all elements of take-off, flight and landing as listed in the section 'Stride Jump Technique'.

Required for a group of 5, to practise take-off and flight movements:
1 'aerobic' step approximately 20 centimetres high.
1 gym mat or sand pit.

Required for a group of 5, to practise landing:
1 'aerobic' step approximately 20 centimetres high.
1 sand pit.

Other Ideas

Sand castles or low sand walls, built sensibly so that they collapse if hit, provide excellent motivation to encourage lift and distance without resorting to constant measurement. It is also great fun!

Teachers and coaches should always remember:
Speed of approach plus lift at take-off determine how far the athlete's centre of gravity will fly. Nothing that is done in the air can alter this fact.

The second objective is to ensure that the body is in the correct position at landing to cut the sand at the furthest possible distance. If long jumpers are able to land with their feet well out in front of them, then they will have made the most of their take-off.

Coaching

The take-off action can be rehearsed by practising 'high skips' or 'long skips' — i.e. complete a sequence of any number between 1 and 10 concentrating on: driving the take-off leg, or driving the free knee upwards, or working the arms correctly, or emphasising the left or right foot take-offs, etc. etc.

5. TRIPLE JUMP (hop-bound-jump)

Triple jumping can be taught efficiently as a class activity and can be taught in an indoor hall.

The initial stages need little or no facilities other than a field of short, smooth, dry grass or a hall and gym mats. Further progress requires a large sand pit.

If all the different varieties and sequences of jumping as listed in the primary section have been covered, the teaching of triple jumping is a simple matter.

Landing forces can be very high in the triple jump. Therefore, sessions should be short and practices should be made from standing or very short approach runs.

WHAT TO TEACH

1. The sequence of hop, bound, jump.
   a) from a standing start position.
   b) from a short run-up.

2. The correct 'even' rhythm of the sequence.

3. Flat foot landings and take-offs.

4. An active take-off, which is the 'reaching and pawing' manner in which the foot is presented to and struck against the ground during landings and take-offs - to those who can cope!

5. A competitive triple jump from a limited run-up (8/9 strides).

Triple Jump Technique

Within that broad aim the following must also be included:

An accurate run up
Rhythm of each take-off
Action of each take-off
A feeling of correct flight
How to land safely
How to land efficiently.

TRIPLE JUMP TECHNIQUE

The triple jump shall consist of a hop, a bound (step) and a jump made in that order.

Run-Up

The organisation of the triple jump run-up is no different to that of the long jump. Therefore, please read that chapter.

The Hop (The same foot must be used to take off and land)

The competent athlete will gather for the hop in the final two strides and take off driving the alternate knee vigorously upwards along with the opposite arm. The take-off leg is extended explosively. Research tells us that the best triple jumpers take off at an angle of 15°-18°. The athlete should sense a flat footed contact with the take-off board, although in actual fact it will be slightly heel first.

During the flight, which must be balanced, the take-off knee is picked up so that the thigh is parallel to the ground. The athlete is then in a position to reach and strike so as to engage the 'active' landing and take off for the second phase.

The Bound or Step (The landing must be made on the other foot from take-off)

The athlete can use a single or double arm action (shift), but must drive the free thigh vigorously so that once again it becomes parallel with the ground. The athlete often appears to demonstrate a splits position in the air when the action is completed properly. Take-off angle 13°-15°.

The Jump

Momentum at this stage is dropping rapidly, however much the athlete strives to maintain it. A double arm shift should be used and, as in all jumps, the free knee should be driven hard and the take-off leg extended explosively. The jump, if long enough, can be completed with any of the recognised long jump techniques. However, beginners are unlikely to have enough time in the air for such luxuries, and a 'stride' or 'hang' style is adequate. The aim of the flight is to adopt a position in the air that will allow for an effective landing. That is, with legs fully extended in front, and with the arms high above the head so that they can be swung downward and backwards. This action lifts the feet just prior to landing because of the principle of Newton's 3rd Law of Motion — to every action there is an equal and opposite reaction. Take-off angle should be higher than in the other two phases - between 20° and 24°.

Rhythm

The rhythm of the sequence of the three jumps is vitally important to gaining good distances. The athlete should attempt to make the flight time of each jump more or less equal. The athlete should therefore sense a TAA – TAA – TAA timing. Beginners often demonstrate a huge hop, a very short step, followed by a long jump! This pattern has been proved to be highly inefficient.

In reality, the best distance ratio for a good triple jumper should be approximately:

Hop   37%   Step   30%   Jump   33%

Arm Actions

Jumpers are able to help their performances by swinging their arms at take-off. The arms can be swung together. This is called a double arm shift. Alternatively, they can be swung one forward and one backward as in a natural running action, a single arm shift. At take-off this arm swing adds lift, or upward momentum, to the athlete. In a single arm shift, even the arm lifted backwards is being driven upwards and consequently adds lift.

A two arm shift is probably more effective but unfortunately takes longer to complete. The hop needs to be completed at the greatest possible speed, and therefore many good triple jumpers use a single arm shift to aid the hop take-off. The jumper will slow and is in a position to use either arm action for the step take-off. However, by the time the athlete takes off for the jump, momentum will have been reduced to such an extent that every acceptable method will be required to maximise that jump, and a two arm shift is likely to be best.

HOW TO TEACH

The whole class can be introduced to the event, but pupils must always work in the same direction and be reasonably well spaced.

The sequence of hop, bound, jump can be taught by (a) the challenge approach or (b) the command method. It is easy for pupils to become confused if directions are not simple and clear.

(a) The Challenge Approach

Challenge the group to follow these exact commands.

Can you leap from standing as follows?:-

1. Left foot to two feet to right foot to two feet ('hop scotch').

2. Can you ensure a bouncy, even rhythm?

3. Left foot to left foot to right to right to left to left (even rhythm)

4. Right to right to left to left and so on

5. Left to left to left to two feet

6. Right to right to right to two feet

7. Left to right to left to right to two feet

8. Right to left to right to left to two feet

9. Left to left to left to right to two feet

10. Right to right to right to left to two feet

11. Left to left to right to two feet

12. Right to right to left to two feet

Avoid telling the pupils your intentions at the beginning. You might label it a fun intelligence test. Ask them what they have done at the end.

AVOID USING THE WORD STEP AT ALL COSTS! If, at the conclusion, you call the sequence hop, bound, jump, the pupils will invariably demonstrate the correct rhythm. Use 'step' and they will not!

(b) The Command Approach

1. Demonstrate a hop from the left foot to the left foot. Copy.

Note: It is worth identifying a very capable pupil and teaching him/her individually prior to the lesson. Use this pupil to ensure accurate demonstrations.

2. Demonstrate a hop on the left foot followed by a big bound. The bound must be of the same height and rhythm as the hop. Copy and practise.

Note: Some pupils might have difficulty in making quick progress. Ensure each instruction can be accomplished successfully before progressing. Time spent on achieving a good hop/bound combination will be time well spent.

3. Demonstrate a hop on the left foot, followed by a bound, followed by a jump to land on two feet. Each movement must be of the same height and rhythm as the hop. Command - LEFT-LEFT-RIGHT-TOGETHER. Copy and practise.

4. Offer the alternative RIGHT-RIGHT-LEFT-TOGETHER as some pupils will be better at the event this way round.

Note: Some pupils may identify with the alternative command: from LEFT to SAME-OTHER-BOTH.

5. Provide lines (the lines of the track) or gym mats, equally spaced, for practice.

A grid can be marked for teaching and practice:-

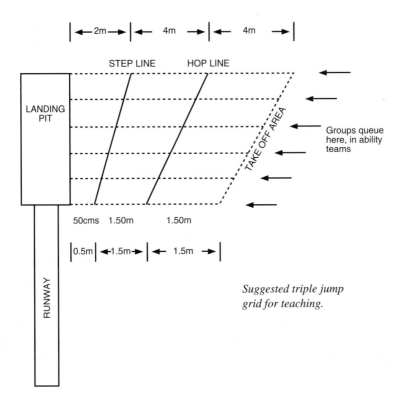

Suggested triple jump grid for teaching.

Pupils should assemble in ability groups, but can progress to wider spaced lines as they progress. However, there is a drawback in that pupils will look down at the lines, spoiling good jumping posture; the trunk should be upright and the hips under the trunk. Watch carefully to see this fault does not develop.

6. Gradually, as pupils master the sequence of movements but before longer distances are attempted, encourage flat foot landings and take-offs. Landings made on the balls of the feet are highly unstable and injury may occur.

7. Teach the 'reaching and pawing' action of the lower leg during landing and take-off. This can be done over a series of six to eight large steps or in the step phase of skipping (hop/step, hop/step, etc.).

During flight the lower leg is extended forward. On approach to and during landing, the leg is swept backwards to minimise shock and also to maximise forward momentum.

Reaching and pawing.

This is not the easiest activity to teach! It is best taught from an accurate demonstration followed by practice and feedback.

2. Introduce a measured run-up

The next task is to move to the runway proper and jump with a measured run-up. It has been explained that landing forces increase drastically when the athletes jump after a fast approach run. At this stage of teaching, athletes who have weak legs and who could collapse with the strain must be restricted to a short approach.

Another problem may arise in that the take-off board could be too far away from the pit for some, just right for others, yet too near for others. The answer is a take-off area marked in chalk one metre square. Do not worry too much about a take-off board in the initial stages as it often causes pupils to look down, spoiling jumping posture.

For detailed instructions on assembling a run-up see the long jump chapter.

6. HIGH JUMP

The introductory stage to successful high jumping is the scissors jump.

This is a very simple activity, needing very little in the way of facilities or knowledge. However, a correct introduction to it and regular practice of it can be extremely beneficial to the most efficient method of jumping high, the 'Fosbury' Flop. (See 'SPECIFIC SAFETY' at the end of this chapter).

All children can scissors jump after a simple introduction. It can be taught indoors in a hall and initially onto gym mats because of its foot-first landing. (However, gym mats are not a suitable situation for any form of competition or trial for height!)

The scissors is an acceptable but not the most efficient competition technique.

The flop technique is very rewarding to practise and teach, but must only be performed on a correct high jump mat due to its 'back drop' type landing.

It is important to note that the rules of high jumping insist that the jump is made from one foot!

WHAT TO TEACH

1. The scissors jump from a standing position to land in a standing position.
2. The scissors jump from a short approach to clear an elastic bar.
3. The flop technique from 5, 7 or 9 stride approach.
4. The correct foot position at take-off.

Scissors.

Within these broad aims the following must also be included:

An accurate run-up (curved for the flop)
Rhythm of take-off
Action of take-off
A feeling of correct flight over the cross bar
A safe landing

THE SCISSORS JUMP TECHNIQUE

Run-up

The start should be from standing, for accuracy.
An odd number of strides might be the easiest to adopt, in which case:
The first foot to move is the eventual take-off foot.
The run should accelerate progressively until the last two strides.
The last two strides into take-off are made with a definite de-daa rhythm.
The run-up should be straight.
The approach should be made at an acute angle to the bar — about 20 degrees.

Take-off

The take-off spot should enable the jumper to clear the bar at its lowest point of sag.
The jump is made from the outside foot.
The jump is made facing the far upright.
The take-off foot should point towards the far upright.
Posture .... upright, head tall.
Arms .... driven upwards, together.
Free leg .... (leading leg) swung upwards and over the bar.
Take-off leg .... extended explosively.

Flight

Posture .... upright.
Free leg .... steps sideways over the bar.
Take-off leg .... is lifted over afterwards.

Landing

Is made on the free or none take-off leg to stand.

HOW TO TEACH

The best method of teaching the scissors is to copy a correct demonstration.

Required — dry, flat take-off surface.
— one well dug sand pit or gym mat per group of 8-10 pupils.
— high jump uprights or similar and an elastic cross bar for each group.

(The gym mat should not be so soft as to enable twisted ankles to occur.)

PROGRESSIONS

Set the elastic bar at a very low height — 20 centimetres.
1. Scissors from a standing start.
2. Scissors from a 3, then from a 5 stride approach.
3. Practise from both sides (take-off legs).
4. Choose favourite side and practise (encourage a vigorous upwards arm swing. Raise the bar gradually and sensibly so that good technique is encouraged, not forgotten.)

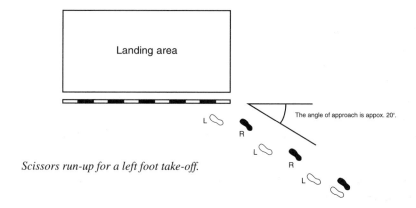

Scissors run-up for a left foot take-off.

Continued and regular practice will improve coordination, strength and awareness.

Pupils must be given the opportunity to attempt a jump from both directions and allowed to practise from their favourite side.

Class control — the teacher must direct the order of jumping; perhaps those on the left jump first, followed by those on the right.

THE FLOP TECHNIQUE

Run-up

The start should be from standing, for accuracy.
An odd number of strides is easiest to adopt.
The first foot to move is the eventual take-off foot.
The run should accelerate progressively until the last two strides.
The last two strides into take-off are made with a definite de-daa rhythm.
The run-up should be J shaped. The first 4 strides should be in a straight line; the final 5 strides should be run on a curve. (Some experts suggest the last 3 strides should be run on a curve.)

Take-off

The take-off spot should enable the jumper to clear the bar at its lowest point of sag.
The jump is made from the outside foot.
The take-off foot should point towards the far upright.
Posture .... upright, head tall.
Arms .... driven upwards, together.
Take-off leg .... extended explosively.
Free leg .... (leading leg) driven knee first upwards.

Flight

It is important to jump 'UP' before clearance is considered!
During flight the athlete completes half a twist to clear the bar head first on the back.
During bar clearance the back should be arched.
In the final stages of bar clearance the body position is changed to a half piked position to enable the heels to clear the bar and also to adopt a safe landing position.

Landing

The landing is made on the back as in a trampoline back drop.

Fosbury Flop.

HOW TO TEACH

The flop should be taught in a small group (6-10) situation while the other members of the class undertake tasks of previously learned activities.

The flop should only be taught by the direct method with the teacher responsible for feedback.

Required — A standard foam high jump landing mat.
          — dry, flat take-off surface.
          — high jump uprights and elastic cross bar.
          — a tall marker to sight. A body will do!.

PROGRESSIONS

Introduce a curved run-up

1. Practise running around a circle; a centre circle of a football pitch is ideal. Run tall leaning inwards from the ankles only. Run both ways.

2. Mark or draw a J-shaped line on the floor for the pupils to follow.

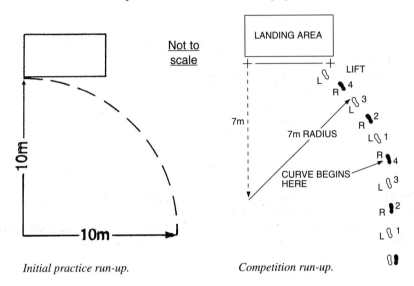

Initial practice run-up.   *Competition run-up.*

Do not insist the line is followed exactly. Allow pupils to make their own personal adjustments to suit their physique, speed and skill. Taller, faster pupils will wish to run a wider curve than shorter, slower pupils.

Practise from 3 strides, then 5 strides, then 7 strides, then 9 strides.

Do not teach a semi-circular run-up. Teach a 1/4 circle, then a J-shaped run-up.

Jump with a 1/2 turn.

Method 1

1. From a short run (3-5 strides), scissors the crossbar to land on the mat in a seat drop facing the far upright (where the marker is placed).

2. Move the marker 20 degrees towards the centre of the run-up area — see diagram. Run and scissors, but turn in the air to land in a seat drop facing the marker.

3. Gradually move the marker towards the centre of the run-up area, so that eventually the jumpers must make a 90° turn in the air to align themselves with the marker before landing in the seat drop.

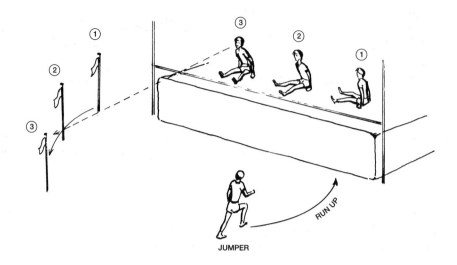

Method 2

Stack the sections of the high jump mat on top of one another to just above head height.

From a short run (3-5 strides), jump up and turn to land upper back and shoulders on the topmost section.

Approach the mat from about 45 degrees and jump from the outside foot.

Teach a back drop landing

1. Stand facing away from the mat, heels about 30 centimetres from the mat.

2. From two feet jump gently up and back to land on the landing area on the 'round' of the back.

3. As confidence and competence improve jump up and over a gradually raised elastic bar, arching the body to clear and piking to land.

Backdrop landing.

Note: It is important to finish this activity with a few one-footed scissors jumps before progressing further, otherwise some of the pupils will move on to the next stage and attempt to jump from two feet!

Practise the complete Flop action

The flop can be practised from 3, 5, 7 and 9 strides. It would be sensible to return frequently to all of the introductory activities and practise them also. A good flop technique is not easy to perfect and these activities will help the pupils orientate themselves.

SPECIFIC SAFETY

1. Take-off

Repeated practice of high jumping from a badly positioned take-off foot will result in injury. The take-off foot should be planted heel first before rolling onto the ball of the foot and should be **pointing towards the direction the jump will take — between the uprights.** It is acceptable if the foot points towards the far upright, because few people have straight legs and feet!

Take-off foot.

It is not acceptable for the athlete to continuously turn the take-off foot outwards, away from the landing area, to assist the turn required in the flop technique. This does not mean avoid teaching the flop. It means teach it correctly.

A non-slip take-off surface and stable shoes are essential. Better high jumpers use heel spikes.

2. Landing areas

Proper high jump landing areas are made of plastic foam. The foam is layered in levels of specific density — soft at the top to break the fall, but hard at the bottom to prevent the athlete hitting the floor. Gymnastic 'crash mats' are not a suitable alternative to the correct facility, and landing on them in a sitting position or back drop could possibly result in serious injury.

3. High jump cross bars

It is advisable that high jump is taught using soft, stretchy, elasticated cross bars. They present no problems, either physically or psychologically. However, it is vital to make certain the uprights cannot topple over onto the athlete when the elastic is stretched between them.

Competition high jump cross bars are rigid and hard. When dislodged, these cross bars remain proud of the landing area and in extreme situations can cause bruising and other injuries if hit or landed upon. For this reason, 'old fashioned' triangular bars should never be used.

7. POLE VAULT

Pole vaulting should be taught 'as near to the ground as possible'! (See 'SPECIFIC SAFETY' at the end of this chapter).

The introductory stage to successful pole vaulting is to learn to swing on a rigid pole.

It can be introduced as a class activity, and most of the essential skills can be taught without access to an expensive pole vault facility. It can be introduced in an indoor hall.

Pole vaulting is best introduced to children of between 9 and 13 years of age, but can be introduced later.

WHAT TO TEACH

1. How to swing on a pole safely.

2. How to swing on a pole effectively.

TEACH 'SWINGING FOR DISTANCE'

Within these broad aims the following must also be included:

Run-up and take-off
⎧ Pole grip
⎪ Pole carry
⎨ An accurate run-up
⎪ A correct pole plant action
⎩ The take-off and pole push

Gymnastic element
⎰ The turn
⎱ A safe landing

THE POLE VAULT TECHNIQUE

(For a right-handed vaulter. Reverse for left-handers.)

Gripping the pole

Grip the pole with the favourite hand at the top, and the other hand between forty and fifty centimetres lower down. The thumbs and forefingers of each hand must be to the top.

Pole carry

RIGHT-HANDED VAULTERS SHOULD CARRY THE POLE ON THEIR RIGHT.

Carrying a pole is an inconvenience. Keep this inconvenience to a minimum by carrying the pole as vertically as possible to begin. As the run-up progresses, allow the pole to fall gradually until two strides from take-off the pole is exactly horizontal. This moment represents the beginning of the 'pole plant'.

However, it is important to appreciate that the run-up, pole-plant and take-off are one progressive movement.

Run-up

The start should be from standing, for accuracy.
An even number of strides should be adopted.
The first foot to move is the right (non take-off) foot.
The run should accelerate progressively until the last two strides.
The last two strides into take-off are made with a galloping (daa-de) rhythm.

Pole-plant

This is a sequence of well rehearsed movements, designed to transfer the pole from the carrying position to an overhead position while placing it into the box or trough for take-off. The right hand moves from above the hip to directly overhead in a vertical line, passing the forehead on the penultimate foot contact. Both hands should push the pole upwards together.

Take-off

RIGHT-HANDED VAULTERS SHOULD TAKE OFF FROM THEIR LEFT FOOT.

At the moment of take-off, the top of the top hand should be vertically aligned with the front of the take-off foot.

The take-off should be identical to that in the long jump, except that the arms are required to push the pole to the vertical.

Swing and Flight

RIGHT-HANDED VAULTERS SHOULD SWING UP THE RIGHT HAND SIDE OF THE POLE. (The pole should be on the vaulter's left.)

Our beginner pole vaulter should concentrate on swinging on the pole from a straight top arm. The free knee should be kept up, and the take-off leg swung up to it. At the last moment the hips can be swivelled to effect a 180° turn to clear the bar. Advanced pole vaulters push the pole back so that it does not knock the bar off. Beginner vaulters are advised to use an elastic crossbar and hang on to the pole until landing.

Landing

Landings into sand or on to a gym mat should be made on the feet. Landings made on to proper landing areas should be made on the back, so that ankles are not twisted.

HOW TO TEACH

The pole vault should be taught in a small group (4-8) situation, while the other members of the class undertake tasks of previously learned activities.

The pole vault should only be taught by the direct method with the teacher responsible for feedback.

PROGRESSIONS

1. Swing on the pole

Teaching Method 1 (Group)

Required   — dry, flat grass or non-slip gym mats (indoor hall).
             — short (2.5 metres) sturdy poles.
             — then: a large sand pit.

In groups of three, spaced 5/10 metres apart, work in one direction only and walk back carrying the pole carefully.

Show and practise the correct grip.

Hold the pole with the top (favourite) hand at forehead height. Carry the pole with top hand at forehead level and the bottom tip close to the ground. Take a few short steps, place the pole on the ground vertically and make a short, controlled swing. Land on the feet.

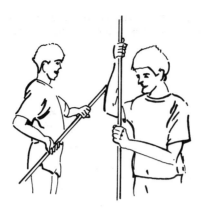

Note: It is important that the pole is vertical at take-off from all viewpoints, not just when viewing from the side; otherwise the vaulter will drift left or right.

Practise until the pupils can comfortably take their bodyweight on the pole.

THIS ACTIVITY IS RELATED TO SAFETY RATHER THAN TO EFFECTIVE POLE VAULTING. THEREFORE, **AS SOON AS THE PUPILS HAVE CONTROL OF THIS ACTIVITY, TEACH THEM TO SWING FROM A STRAIGHT TOP ARM:**

Take a grip of the pole vertically as high as possible from tiptoe. Carry the pole high above the head with a straight top arm. Take a few short steps, place the pole on the ground close to the pupil's take-off foot vertically and make a short, controlled swing. Land on the take-off foot.

Place lines on the floor one metre apart. Vault across this 'stream'. The pole is allowed to be placed in the 'stream'.

Very gradually extend the width of the lines up to two metres.

Move to a sand pit.

Grip the pole 20 centimetres higher than previously to accommodate the pole sinking into the sand. Once the pupil has practised sufficiently to be controlled, raise the grip by TWO CENTIMETRES AT A TIME — no faster. Gradually extend the distance of the swing.

Teach the pole-plant action.

1. Stand square to the front with the left foot forward.
2. The pole should be held horizontally, the favourite (top) hand under the armpit.
3. 'Uppercut' both hands so that the favourite hand is at the forehead. (Do not twist the head to sight along the pole.)
4. Step forward on to the right foot.
5. Push the pole upwards to arm's length, step on to the left 'take-off' foot.
6. Bring the free knee through to 45 degrees.
7. Relax and repeat many times, first at a walk and then at a jog.
8. Add two walking (jogging) strides before the two plant strides and practise — one/two, one/two.
9. When competent, use and vault into the sand pit from a low, safe hand grip from four strides (2 running, 2 planting).
10. Gradually add two strides at a time to extend the run-up.

Note:

a) Counting the number of strides during practice helps the pupil time the plant. Count — 1, 2, 3, 4, one/two, for a six stride run-up.

b) It is vital to start each lesson with a rehearsal of introductory activities before vaulting or progressing to more difficult practices. Accidents can be caused by gripping too high or by mistiming the pole plant action.

2. Introduce a measured run-up

There are two methods of organising a measured run-up.

Method 1

Run back, carrying the pole, from the take-off spot. A partner counts the strides and spots the footmark at however many strides is agreed, 4, 6, or 8. Remember to move the non take-off foot first.

Method 2

Assemble the run-up gradually using the following format:

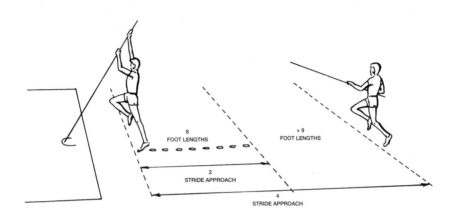

Measure back from the take-off spot 8 foot-lengths. Mark.
From the mark run 2 natural steps and take off.

Measure back from the take-off spot 8 foot-lengths and a further 9 foot-lengths (17 in total). Mark.
From the mark, run 4 natural strides and vault.

And so on.

Once understood, this latter method provides the ideal progressive practice situation. It is also simpler and safer to use this method to establish a run-up on a full facility which has a proper pole vault 'box' into which the pole is to be planted.

3. Swing/Flight/Turn and Land

The swing or hang should be made with the favourite (upper) arm straight. Rope swinging is a super introductory activity, especially if the pupil can initiate a hip swivel turn at the end of each swing. The beginner turn on the pole is the same.

Teaching Method 2 (Individual)

Required   — rigid sturdy pole, 3+ metres long.
               — a large, well dug, sand pit.
               — dry flat run-up.
Once the teacher is confident the pupil can control his/her bodyweight on the pole, the pupil attempts to vault from two strides immediately.

However, the teacher 'stands in', grips the pole and ensures the pole reaches the vertical by pulling it if necessary. When the pole has reached the vertical with the pupil hanging from it, the teacher manually 'shapes' the pupil to the correct position.

The pole is placed into the sand pit at take-off.

A shallow, 'box' shaped hole is scooped from the sand pit to identify the point of pole plant.

The pupil should grip the pole 50 centimetres higher than can be reached when the pole is held vertically. (Do not place in the sand to make this measurement.)

The pole is gripped with the favourite hand highest and the other hand about 20-30 centimetres lower.

The pupil stands at the approximate point of take-off and places the pole in the sand 'box'. The pole is held as high as possible above the pupil's head and the exact point of take-off is identified.

The PUPIL then measures back 8 foot-lengths and makes this the point of start to the two stride run up.

The pupil holds the pole high above the head with the tip near the ground.

The pupil takes two strides and takes off, pushing the pole to the vertical at take-off.

The teacher stands in the sand pit by the point of pole plant and grips the pole with the left hand (for a right-handed vaulter) as the pupil takes off. The left hand then helps pull the pole to the vertical, if necessary. The right hand is used to control and shape the pupil.

The active part of the exercise is completed when the pupil is hanging from the pole with a straight top arm, chest to the pole, free knee high and take-off leg held back.

The pupil is then lowered in a controlled manner to the ground.
The activity is progressed by:

1. Holding the pole at forehead height to begin, and then pushed to arm's length during the last stride.

2. Teaching the pole plant action and vaulting from two strides using this action.

   Note: When the pole plant action is used from two strides, it is important to initiate the arm movement before the first foot moves.

3. Adding two, then four strides to the beginning of the run-up. (For each two strides the vaulter should be able to raise the grip height by 20 centimetres.)

The teacher must gradually ensure the pupil can undertake the activity with less and, finally, no support.

4. Teach a hip swivel turn and bar clearance.

SPECIFIC SAFETY

1. Ensure the beginner does not grip the pole too high.

2. Progress carefully. Mistakes can result in falls, and the landing area and surrounding area should be able to accommodate these without resulting problems. A full size landing area presents problems to the beginner because it is too high. Remove all loose objects from the surrounding area — hurdles, rakes, etc. and cover hard edges to sand pits with rubber gym mats.

3. Proper pole vault landing areas are made of plastic foam. The foam is layered in levels of specific density — soft at the top to break the fall but hard at the bottom to prevent the athlete hitting the floor. Gymnastic 'crash mats' are not a suitable alternative to the correct facility, and landing on them in a sitting position or back drop could result in serious injury.

   Always check the condition of the landing area, especially to see that there are no gaps underneath the cover through which the athlete may fall.

4. It is advisable that pole vault is taught using soft, stretchy, elasticated cross bars. They present no problems, either physically or psychologically. However, it is vital to make certain the uprights cannot topple over onto the athlete when the elastic is stretched between them.

   Competition pole vault cross bars are rigid and hard. When dislodged, these cross bars remain proud of the landing area and in extreme situations can cause bruising and other injuries if hit or landed upon. For this reason, 'old fashioned' triangular bars should never be used.

5. No one should take part in a competition until they have proved themselves reasonably proficient at the activity.

Important

The learning of pole vault is a young person's activity if success at the very highest level is desired, as with gymnasts or musicians. Such potential internationals require individual coaching which is beyond the scope of this booklet. If you wish to become involved in the preparation of top class pole vaulters or have identified someone who deserves such coaching, contact your Regional Expert or phone the Coaching Department on 0121 456 5098.

8. SAFETY IN JUMPS

What was a moral obligation has in recent years become a legal obligation. To all teachers and coaches of sport, athletes and administrators, safety is a way of life, an awareness developed to a fine art over long years of experience. An eye which surveys every facility, piece of equipment, practice, exercise and technique without undermining the confidence of the performer. An ability not just to spot danger, but to spot danger and act upon it before it causes damage ("foreseeability").

This is no help to the beginner teacher. In fact, no sensitive, intelligent human would undertake such activities were he to dwell on the problems without knowing the joy and educational value athletics can bring. However, having decided to undertake such responsibility, he or she would do well to study the following with care:

1. Philosophy

A correct coaching philosophy goes a long way to ensuring a caring attitude, appreciating that the aim is to do one's best for the whole person, not just the competitive and physical aspects of the pupil.

2. Get yourself qualified

. . . and understand the underlying concepts as well as the knowledge you intend to pass on. Avoidance of injury is very much part of a coaches' code of safety. Warm ups are essential, and care is essential when working on such activities as mobility, strength (particularly weight training) and specific techniques. It is not enough just to have "in depth" knowledge of the activities; you must also know in which order they should be practised, e.g. always practise skills before doing stamina training etc.

Always coach within your understanding and err on the side of caution. There is a well organised coach education structure with National Coaches and Area Event Coaches only too willing to provide the experience. Use them!

3. Operate within the regulations

UK Athletics and the English Schools A.A. publish positive guidelines on how athletics can be practised without danger to life and limb. Each event has its own problems, particularly the high jump and pole vault. The list of all the safety factors is lengthy, but they are included in the relevant event-specific publication. Remember it is not enough for the javelin group to be aware of their own problems — so must all the other groups working in the vicinity.

NB: The excellent safety chapter in the Club Coach Level 1 Manual.

4. Teach or Coach within your limitations

It is important that the coach has an accurate opinion of his ability in:

a) Knowledge
b) Coaching and teaching technique
c) Crowd control.

Experienced coaches can manage large groups and still maintain adequate supervision. The beginner coach should not take on such large groups until experience has been gained.

5. Provide the safeguards designed to minimise the dangers inherent in a particular activity.

This involves two main factors: (a) the obvious safe facilities, i.e. safe landing areas and other appropriate factors for safety, and (b) individual and group discipline. The coach should arrive first and leave last, especially when dealing with youngsters.

Words spoken to an individual have far more power and effect than those spoken to a group. It is important that the coach or teacher finds his own style of management to enforce good and safe conduct. One that is in accord with his own personality. Watch and quiz the best teachers and coaches around you and adapt techniques learned to your own style. Learn when to speak, when not to speak, how to manipulate your voice (if you shout a lot, what do you do if something very important becomes apparent!). Learn where to stand (and where not) and when to scold and when to praise. Many accidents can be avoided by praise, e.g. Well done Gareth! Look, everyone, notice the way he is always considerate to other track users by . . . I approve. Well done!

6. Inspect equipment regularly and ensure facilities are in good order. Nothing left in jumping pits, no hurdles or rakes near to fall or trip on — once again a thousand possibilities.

Notify the authorities if dangerous conditions exist. Always check equipment away. Hooligans might have other plans for high jump cross bars that have been left out!

7. Provide sufficient instruction to athletes before exposing them to activities. This will be very individual, as will making sure it is within their capabilities. It should be suitable to their age, experience, physique and co-ordination. Mental preparation for the activity will decide success or failure.

8. Do not force athletes to do something they feel is beyond them. Differentiate between encouragement and force.

9. First Aid. Act promptly and with discretion when giving first aid. Take a course on the subject. In case of doubt, follow the rule "ensure no further damage"; get quick and expert help, and know where the nearest telephone is — always.

Beware of questionable practices and do not take on roles for which you are not qualified, e.g. diagnosing injuries or prescribing remedies or medication.

10. Act as a reasonably prudent person and anticipate dangers which would be apparent to the trained and intelligent.

While death and accident attributed to stupidity and incompetence are inexcusable, injuries are inevitable because all activities contain an element of risk. The aim is to minimise this element.

Education of the participants is therefore a very important aspect and CHILDREN LEARN BEST BY COPYING.

Successful and healthy athletics is the harnessing of the enthusiasm, ambition and ability of the young by the experience and judgement of the mature.

9. TEACHING METHODS

TEACHING/COACHING STYLES

There is no one definitive style of teaching. Teaching is a very complex and idiosyncratic affair, and most teachers and coaches adopt various ploys and methods to achieve their ends. Invariably (as they become more experienced), teachers switch from style to style in the process of instruction — possibly without being aware of the switch. Nevertheless, it might be profitable to examine the whole range that is available to the teacher/coach.

(The main reference for focusing upon teaching style is accorded to Muska Motsson in his book "Teaching Physical Education" (2nd edition 1981 pub. Charles Merrill) where he explains this range with the term — "From Command to Discovery". This modification suggests "From Direct – – – (limitations) – – – to Free").

1. Direct Instruction

This is the most common form of instruction, where the teacher/coach makes all the decisions and the individual responds to commands. To be effective, good demonstrations need to be made and there must be productive feedback.

2. Controlled Practice

The individual practises what has been taught, either by verbal instruction or by task cards, and the teacher/coach gives individual feedback.

3. Reciprocal

The pupils teach each other — either from a knowledge base with a verbal instruction or from the observation of well-illustrated visual aids. One person can teach another — or two or three.

Teaching technique is difficult to acquire — the teacher/coach, having given responsibility to a "teacher", does not interfere — but goes to the "teacher" and asks and makes comments about what is happening.

4. Self Checking

The pupil has a certain amount of knowledge and is able to check from a task card which contains a number of key points. The pupil works on these "qualitatively", from a series of key tasks relating to an event, and checks them off as and when they are achieved. One would assume that simple schedules would come under this category and the many measurements that athletes are entrusted to make about their own performance. Although the initial task is the product of the teacher/coach, within this style there is more freedom on the part of the pupils to be responsible for their own learning.

5. Individual Choice

The coach provides a range of activities within the event and the athletes make a choice according to their assessment of their capabilities. There may be a range of throwing implements or ways of throwing, a range of jumping activities or a range of running schedules. This style requires meticulous preparation and sometimes the athletes overestimate what they can do, especially with running tasks. However, having experienced difficulty, it is often a salutary learning episode.

6. Questioning

This can be via the coach asking questions about range and force — and should happen AS THE EVENT IS PRACTISED. Sometimes this type of style is referred to as Guided Discovery. Each subsequent question funnels the response down to the "correct" answer and it can tend to become too verbal. I like to employ this type of questioning with regard to some stage teaching where the last part of the skill is taught first, e.g. the long jump — first from standing — then from a short run — "Why did you go further?" is highly related to the improvement and is likely to elicit a response that will show UNDERSTANDING. It can be applied to large groups but is very effective on a one to one basis. The coach is leading the athlete to become aware of the purpose and meaning of the event.

Another type of questioning can reverse the "funnel" and lead the athlete to discover OTHER WAYS instead of one way. This is sometimes referred to as Problem Solving. Whereas by this method the athlete would "arrive" at a state of understanding through finding different ways and help in the application of techniques to solve problems in other areas, it would not help directly in the learning of skills. It might also be dangerous with regard to some jumping events: Fosbury Flop and Pole Vault.

7. Free Choice

This, one would hope, would be the situation where the athlete would be developing independence — using the teacher/coach as adviser and consultant. One would imagine this utopian scene at a school where those that have opted to do athletics — choose their own events — are responsible for their own organisation and have respect for safe practices — even to the point of organising their own competitions.

Adapted from 'Junior Athletics, Methods of Teaching and Coaching', by Dave Edgecombe.

HIGH JUMP
An activity for 4 to 8 persons

You need: Flexibar   Clipboard and result sheet
'Easily read' 5 cm markers (with coloured tape) on High Jump or Badminton stands

---

TEAM OR PARTNER COMPETITION   A v B

SET THREE STANDARDS – eg:

       1m 10 =   5 points
       1m 20 = 10 points
       1m 30 = 20 points

METHOD

       A's jump in rotation while
       B's officiate and record

       As many 'goes' as you like

       2 mins/3 mins/4 mins each team

Same method:-

       Standing jump competition

       3 stride competition

10. RULES FOR COMPETITION

It is very important that competitors, and therefore teachers and coaches, know the rules of their competition thoroughly. The rules are there to ensure each athlete knows exactly what to expect, and that all have a fair chance. Those athletes that do not know the rules put themselves at a disadvantage.

The International Amateur Athletic Federation Handbook contains all the rules for international competition.

However, it is not unusual for countries or area associations to have their own version of the rules for domestic competition and it is important to have a copy of these also.

A handbook called 'Rules for Competition' contains the official version of the rules applied by UK Athletics.

The rules are occasionally changed if they become outdated or inappropriate and it is important to possess an up-to-date version.

It is a simple matter to buy a copy of the rules. They may be on sale at athletics bookshops at major competitions or they can be bought from the official Athletics Bookcentre. Please see the list of useful addresses at the end of this chapter.

The following is a summary of the important rules likely to affect this level of athletics.

Long Jump

A run up of unlimited length is allowed. The jumper must take off from behind a scratch line. A take-off board is provided, made of wood and set into the ground flush with the run up. The front edge of this board marks the scratch line and soft material is laid beyond the line to help the judges ensure no one contravenes the rule. The jumper lands in a pit of sand, raked level with the run up. The jump is measured from the scratch line to the nearest indentation made in the sand to the scratch line by any part of the jumper's body. Once the jump has been made, the jumper must leave the sand pit under control and must leave it beyond the mark made. The jumper is not allowed any assistance such as springs in the shoes or weights in the hand.

Triple Jump (Hop, Step and Jump)

The three phases must be continuous and made in the following order:

Hop   —   The landing must be made on the same foot as was used to take off.

Step   —   The opposite foot must be used for landing as was used for take off.

Jump   —   Any controlled form of landing is acceptable.

The competition layout is the same as for the long jump; however, the scratch line and take-off board will be set at an appropriate distance from the sand pit. This may be 7 metres, 9 metres, 11 metres or 13 metres, depending on the standard of the competition.

High Jump

A cross-bar is set on two uprights at ever increasing heights and the athlete that jumps over the bar set at the greatest height, without knocking it off, is declared the winner. A large flat area, known as the fan, is provided for an unlimited run up and a landing area or bed made of soft plastic foam provides safety on landing. There are very specific rules governing the size and composition of the landing areas allowed for competition.

The organisers will decide the starting height, and the heights to which the bar will be raised. For example, the competition may start at 1.30 metres and then be raised a further 5 centimetres at the end of each round until everyone is eliminated.

Each athlete is allowed three attempts at each height and is eliminated from the competition when he has incurred three consecutive failures. Athletes do not have to attempt each height nor do they have to take all three attempts at the same height. This can lead to tactics! However, they cannot go back down a height, nor can they attempt a height once they have declared they will pass.

The athlete must jump from one foot. Two footed jumps are not allowed. If the bar wobbles for a long time and finally falls off it is the judge who decides whether the jump was fair or a failure.

A jump is also considered a failure if the athlete touches the ground beyond the plane of the uprights without having cleared the bar first. The bar is always measured at its lowest point and to the nearest whole centimetre below.

If an athlete wins by clearing a height when all other competitors have failed, he may then continue jumping and choose the height to which the bar shall be raised.

Pole Vault

The pole must be made of one piece and can be of any material. A rubber or plastic bung is allowed to be placed on the end of the pole to protect it. The pole vaulter can use sticky substances and/or up to two layers of tape to help the grip!

The method of competition is the same as the high jump.

The run-up is unlimited and a sunken box, 20 centimetres deep, is built into the end of the run-up in which the vaulter places the pole at take-off. This stops the pole from slipping away. A bar is placed on two uprights but the uprights can be moved, up to 80 centimetres forward or 40 centimetres backwards from the plane of the back of the box.

A large safe landing area must be used and the size of this landing area is strictly controlled by the athletics authorities. The very minimum size for competition is one that is 5 metres square with added front extensions. Almost all international competitions are held on landing areas larger than this minimum size. The bed must also be thick enough to stop the vaulter 'bottoming out' or hitting the floor through the bed.

The pole vaulter is not allowed to climb the pole.

A trial is not recorded until the vaulter or the pole breaks the vertical plane of the back of the box, e.g. the vaulter may stop during the run-up, return to the starting point and begin the vault again.

Also:

Clothing: The athlete must wear a vest and a pair of shorts or the equivalent and they must remain decent if they get wet.

Number of attempts: Long jump and triple jump competitors are allowed between three and six individual trials in 'an order of competition' decided by the organisers and announced in advance. The high jumpers and pole vaulters are allowed three attempts at each height and are eliminated from the competition when they have incurred three consecutive failures. The results will be recorded on a card designed for the purpose.

Winning: By jumping the highest/furthest; but should there be a tie, which is not infrequent in the high jump, the result is referred. In the horizontal jumps the person who has the second best effort is declared the winner. In the vertical jumps, the winner is the competitor with the lowest number of jumps/vaults at the height at which the tie occurs. If the tie still remains, the competitor with the lowest total of failures throughout the competition is awarded the higher place.

Order of jumping: A draw will be made by the organisers and athletes are told the competition order before the start.

Must numbers be worn? If the organisers provide them. Every athlete must wear two numbers, one on the chest and one on the back — except the pole vaulters and high jumpers who need only wear one.

Personal equipment: Pole vaulters who possess their own vaulting poles do not have to share their poles with other competitors.

Time per attempt: The athlete is not allowed to keep everyone waiting for an unreasonable amount of time. In fact, each trial should be completed within one minute. Once again, pole vaulters have a dispensation and are allowed one and a half minutes.

Run-up markers: It is best to put a marker alongside the runway, something that cannot be accidentally kicked away. High jumpers should use sticky tape. If in doubt, check with the official looking after the competition.

Coaching assistance during the competition: Once the competition starts the athlete is not allowed to communicate with the coach.

What if the vaulting pole breaks? It is important that the competition is conducted fairly. Therefore, if the pole breaks the athlete is not penalised and is allowed that attempt again.
